MEANING

of

COFFEE

Edited by
Jeffrey Young

Author: Allegra Strategies
Design: John Osborne
Researchers: Daniela Falvo, Rebecca Hodgson,
Nicole Miranda and Hana Nessim
Publisher: Allegra Publications Ltd

Dedicated to
Aaron, Adrian, Ashley, Barbara & Erika

Today is a good day
to have a good day.

A yawn is
a silent scream
for coffee.

I'm not a morning person or a night owl. I'm a "whenever my coffee kicks in" person, and then I'm a "need more coffee" person.

The world is a safer place
once I've had my coffee.

Our greatest glory
is not in never falling
but in rising
every time we fall.

CONFUCIUS

TGIFC

– Thank God I Found Coffee.

Women who aspire
to be equal to men
are unambitious.

MARILYN MONROE

Life is about
the people you meet
and the things
you create with them.

HOLSTEE MANIFESTO

On the eighth day,
God created coffee.

If this is coffee,
please bring me some tea.
But if this is tea,
please bring me some coffee.

ABRAHAM LINCOLN

I'm through with love.
Thank God there's
still coffee.

Mothers are those
wonderful people who can
get up in the morning
before the smell of coffee.

Make coffee not war.

Don't let what you can't do
stop you from doing
what you can do.

JOHN WOODEN

If you live to be 100,
I want to be 100 minus
1 day so I never have to
live without you.

WINNIE THE POOH

I am just waiting to see
if my coffee chooses to use
its powers for good
or evil today.

I must get up,
my coffee needs me.

I envy the cup of coffee that gets to kiss your sleepy lips every cold and bitter morning.

SADE ANDRIA ZABALA

Certainly the caffeine in coffee...
is somewhat of a stimulant.
But if you drink it in moderation,
which I think four or five cups
a day is, you're fine.

HOWARD SCHULTZ,
FOUNDER OF STARBUCKS CORPORATION

$$Energy = MilkCoffee^2$$

Coffee:

the most important meal

of the day.

When I read about the
evils of drinking coffee,
I gave up reading.

I tried to behave,
but there were too many
other options.

Forever: time it takes to brew the first pot of coffee in the morning.

Eighty percent of success is showing up.

WOODY ALLEN

Be the change
you wish to see
in the world.

GANDHI

Coffee is why I got out
of bed today.

A life without coffee
is a life not lived.

With every kiss
and every hug,
you make me fall
in love.

We don't stop playing
because we grow old.
We grow old because
we stop playing.

GEORGE BERNARD SHAW

I love you more than coffee
(but please don't make me
prove it).

What will you do today
that will matter tomorrow?

What on earth
could be more luxurious
than a sofa, a book and
a cup of coffee?

ANTHONY TROLLOPE

When was the last time
you did something
for the first time?

Life is not measured
by the number of breaths
that you take but by the
moments that take your
breath away.

MAYA ANGELOU

Give me coffee to change
the things I can
and wine to accept
the things I cannot.

The time to love is now.

LEO BUSCAGLIA

The lab called today
and apparently my blood
type has changed from
'A Positive' to 'Arabica
Mountain Roast'.

Step aside coffee,
this is a job for alcohol.

Unless you realise that you have the power to say 'No', you can never really say 'Yes'.

DAN MILLMAN

(Included For Aphrodite & Cleopatra)

The more you do,
the more you do.

Big things often happen in the little moments.

TOPAZ

Behind every successful woman
is a substantial amount of coffee.

As long as there was coffee
in the world, how bad
could things be?

CASSANDRA CLARE, CITY OF ASHES

Anyone who has never made a mistake has never tried anything new.

ALBERT EINSTEIN

If there ever comes a day
we can't be together,
keep me in your heart and
I'll be there forever.

WINNIE THE POOH

She says: "If you were my husband, I would poison your coffee."

He replies: "If you were my wife, I would drink it."

I am not addicted to coffee.
Yes I drink a lot, it is half of my
calorie intake and is necessary
to stabilize my mood swings.
But I am NOT addicted.

Raisin cookies that look like chocolate chip cookies are the main reason I have trust issues.

Positive thoughts
create positive realities.

BRIT MCINERNEY

Pilates?
O heavens, no!
I thought you said
'pie and lattes.'

Learn from yesterday,

Live for today,

Hope for tomorrow.

ALBERT EINSTEIN

Coffee: because anger
management is way
too expensive.

Given enough coffee,
I could rule the world.

Fact: Coffee drinkers
make better lovers.

If you are looking
for the love of your life, stop;
they will be waiting for you
when you start doing
the things you love.

HOLSTEE MANIFESTO

I like my coffee strong, not lethal.

Sherman T Potter, M*A*S*H

I've learned that people will forget what you said, people will forget what you did, but people will never forget how you made them feel.

MAYA ANGELOU

If asked, 'how do you take your coffee?' I reply, 'seriously, very seriously'.

A good idea will keep you
awake for the morning;
a great idea will keep you
awake at night.

MARILYN VOS SAVANT

You'll always be my friend.
You know too much.

Don't cry because it's over,
smile because it happened.

DR SEUSS

And will you succeed?

Yes! You will, indeed!

(98 and ¾ percent guaranteed).

DR SEUSS,
OH, THE PLACES YOU'LL GO!

Déjà Brew: the feeling that you have had this coffee before.

Live your life happy,
you're a long time dead.

On the bright side,
my coffee won't get cold
in Hell.

Thoughts

Dreams

Plans

Thoughts

Dreams

Plans

Thoughts

Dreams

Plans

Thoughts

Dreams

Plans